Maps and Mapping for Canadian kids

Laura Peetoom & Paul Heersink

Scholastic Canada Ltd.
Toronto New York London Auckland Sydney
Mexico City New Delhi Hong Kong Buenos Aires

Scholastic Canada Ltd.
604 King Street West, Toronto, Ontario M5V 1E1, Canada

Scholastic Inc.
557 Broadway, New York, NY 10012, USA

Scholastic Australia Pty Limited
PO Box 579, Gosford, NSW 2250, Australia

Scholastic New Zealand Limited
Private Bag 94407, Botany, Manukau 2163, New Zealand

Scholastic Children's Books
Euston House, 24 Eversholt Street, London NW1 1DB, UK

Library and Archives Canada Cataloguing in Publication
Peetoom, Laura
Maps and mapping for Canadian kids / Laura Peetoom, Paul Heersink.
Includes index.
ISBN 978-1-4431-0493-7
1. Map reading--Canada--Juvenile literature. 2. Maps--Juvenile
literature. 3. Cartography--Juvenile literature. I. Heersink, Paul II. Title.

GA105.6.P44 2011   j912.01'4   C2011-901360-6

Credits: Cover background: © Tim Pohl/iStockphoto. Cover illustration and page 24: by Ben Hodson © 2011 Scholastic
Canada Ltd. Page ii: © adroach/iStockphoto. Pages 2–38, Pushpins: © Brandon Laufenberg/iStockphoto. Page 2, 6, 8, top:
iStockphoto. Page 2, background: © Jolande Gerritsen/iStockphoto;. Page 3, left: © MIXA(RF)/Getty Images; right: © JGI/
Jamie Grill(RF)/Getty Images. Page 4, top: © Gertjan Hooijer/iStockphoto; bottom: © Joseph Gareri/iStockphoto. Page 5,
top: Photo © Christine Ensing, used by permission; middle: image courtesy Pictometry Canada, Corp. Pages 5, bottom, 7,
8 inset, 9, 11 top, 30, 34, 37: Paul Heersink. Page 8, bottom: © Airphoto-Jim Wark. Pages 10, 12 bottom, 27 bottom:
© Department of Natural Resources Canada. All rights reserved. Page 11 bottom: © Canadian Broadcasting Corporation.
Page 12 top: courtesy Caleb Rzepa Sztainbok; Page 13: Carta marina, opus Olai Magni Gotti Lincopensis, ex typis Antonii
Lafreri Sequani, Rom, 1572 coloured engraving, National Library of Sweden, Map collection, KoB, Kartor, 1 ab. Page 14:
© The Granger Collection, NYC — All rights reserved. Page 15: © The British Library Board, (Selfmark Maps C.18.c.21).
Page 16: Library and Archives Canada, e010764733. Page 17: © William Stewart. Pages 18 and 29: Photos by Paul
Heersink. Page 20: © Stephen Strathdee/ iStockphoto. Page 22, from top: © AlexStar/ iStockphoto; © hepatus/
iStockphoto; © Yuriy Chaban/ iStockphoto; © Stockbyte/Thinkstock; © Diane Labombarbe/iStockphoto. Page 23: Photo
© Canadian Museum of Civilization, 989.56.1, photo Harry Foster, T2003-108. Page 25: Illustration by Dave McKay
© Scholastic Education; bottom: © Jeff Metzger/Shutterstock. Page 26: Photo by Ross MacDonald. Page 27, top: © Canada
Post Corporation 1957. Reproduced with Permission; Page 28: Image Courtesy of University of Manitoba : Archives &
Special Collections. Page 31: The Challenger Map Foundation. Page 33: © Thinkstock Images/Getty Images. Page 35:
courtesy Milena Rzepa Sztainbok. Page 36: Image Parks Canada © 2011 Google, Image NASA Image © 2011 ImageGlobe.
Page 38: © Ingus Evertovskis. © Alexandra Grablewski/Getty Images.

Text copyright © 2011 by Laura Peetoom and Paul Heersink.

6 5 4 3 2 1   Printed in Canada 119   11 12 13 14 15 16

Table of Contents

INTRODUCTION 2

WHAT IS A MAP? 4

GETTING THE PICTURE 6
Scale 6
Symbols 8
Specialty Maps 10
Colour 12

MAPPING CANADA 14

WHERE IN THE WORLD? 18
Cardinal Directions 19
Orientation 20
Navigation 22
GPS Navigation 24

SIZING THINGS UP 29

MAKE YOUR OWN MAP 30
Making a Map 32

SHOWING WHAT WE KNOW 36

GLOSSARY 38

INTRODUCTION

When you go to a new place, do you follow a map?

Maps are pictures of places. They show you how to get around in a place that's unfamiliar, or tell you something new about a place you know. Maps are inspiring: there's nothing like reading a map to make you want to get out and explore!

Maps have an important part in Canada's history. When European explorers came to this land, it was unknown and mysterious to them. They made maps to record what they learned about the new land. These maps inspired others to come and see for themselves.

Maps are *still* important to Canada. Cities and towns keep changing, and we are always learning new things about our land. With new tools for collecting and showing information, maps and mapping keep changing, too.

Each map is unique; even different maps of the same place aren't identical. But all maps share certain basic traits. Understand those, and you will be able to read any map — or make your own.

Let's take a look at maps and mapping in Canada!

WHAT IS A MAP?

Have you ever been on an airplane on a clear day? The plane takes off and the earth seems to drop away. As you go higher, the plane tilts, and you look out the window. The place you just left is spread out below. It looks like a picture, with lines, squares and different-coloured patches — like a map.

A map is a picture of a place, but not like a painting or a photograph, which shows us what a place looks like. A map is a picture of information about a place. A map can tell readers such things as

- how to get to a place and how to get around within it;

- what the land looks like: hilly or flat, with forests, valleys or lakes;

- what services there are: hospitals, schools, shopping malls;

- how many people live there.

There's print on a map (mostly names), but all this information is shown using lines, shading, colours and symbols.

The place you just left felt as big as the world while you were in it. Now, you can cover it with your hand.

4

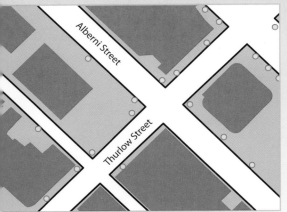

hurlow and Alberni Streets in
ancouver, British Columbia: on the
round, from the air and on a map

A map is a view from above — directly above. Some things disappear, and everything flattens out. It's harder to tell what is high and what is low.

But just like that airplane view, with the details gone, other things become clearer on a map. You get a sense of how far away one place is from another, or how close. And you can see the important features of a place — roads, towns and lakes — completely, not just in bits and pieces.

Sometimes, a simple "airplane" view is all you need. But with maps, it's possible to get that view and more complex information, at the same time. It's all in how you look at it.

FOR THE BIRDS

There are two kinds of overhead views: an airplane view (true overhead) and a bird's-eye view (also called oblique). A bird's-eye view is high, but angled — what an ordinary bird flying about on its daily business would see, or what you might see from the roof of a tall building.

GETTING THE PICTURE

When you look at a map, one or more of these things may jump out at you:

- It fits in your hands, on a table or on a screen. A map is never life-sized; it's always on a smaller **scale**.

- It's full of lines, dots, squares, triangles, shadings, arrows and other **symbols**.

- It has **colour**. Even a one-colour map will have varying shades and areas that are dotted or plain.

Scale, symbols, colour: let's look at these three basic features of a map.

Scale

In a photograph, people are much smaller than they are in real life. But everyone looks "right" to you, even though they may be only a few centimetres high. Why? Because in the picture, the **proportions** are the same as in real life: your little sister still comes up to your waist and your mom is still shorter than your dad. Those proportions stay the same whether the photo fits into a wallet or hangs on a wall, whether it includes the scenery around you or focuses on your happy faces.

Without scale and proportion, things look distorted.

In a similar way, maps shrink the world to different sizes, depending on how much they are meant to show you. But they shrink it all equally, so that everything has the same **relative** distance. How far they shrink the world is called scale.

The **scale bar** on a map tells you if a centimetre on the map is equal to a metre, a kilometre or more in real life. If Maple Street on a map is half as long as Plains Avenue, then Maple Street will be half as long as Plains Avenue in real life.

Scale is not the same as size. The map to the left is on a larger scale than the map below. It shows less of Alberton, Prince Edward Island, but in greater detail. The map below shows more of Alberton and the surrounding area, in less detail.

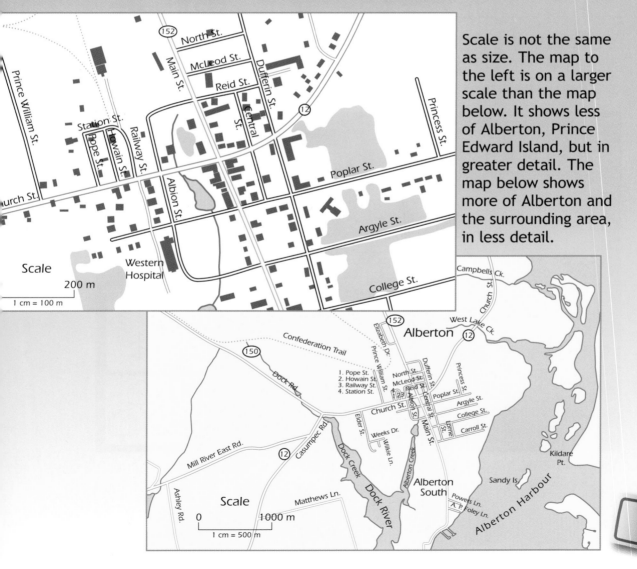

Symbols

Maps are pictures of information about places. And there can be a lot of it. Symbols show information in a way that doesn't take up too much room and is easy to tell apart from other information.

Sometimes symbols look like what they represent. Other symbols are chosen for their simplicity, like dots and circles for towns on a map of your province or territory. The size of the circle represents how big or small the town is.

A symbol conveys information in a clear and instant way.

A mixed forest like this could be shown on a map using symbols.

If you're not sure what a symbol means, you can check a map's **legend**. Common maps, such as road maps, have a standard set of symbols to represent things like major highways or gravel roads, parks, schools, or provincial capitals. If you read enough maps, you'll learn to recognize these without having to consult the legend.

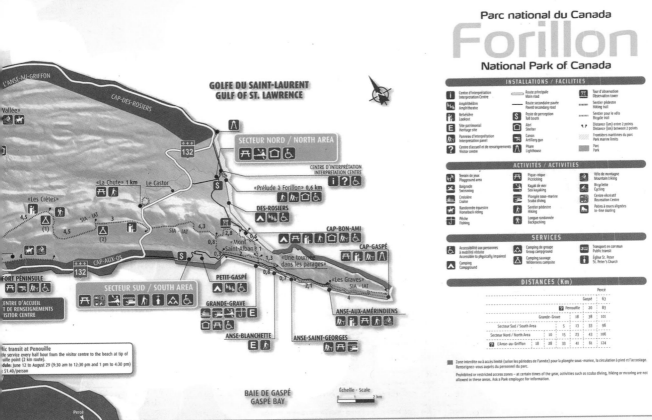

Part of a map and its legend

Specialty Maps

You might need a little extra training to read some maps, which show specific kinds of information using unique families of symbols.

A flat map can show us what's to the right and left, behind and ahead; it can't show what's high and what's low. At least, not without symbols. On a **topographic** map, **contour lines** show this information. The narrower the distance between the lines on the map, the steeper the rise or fall in real life.

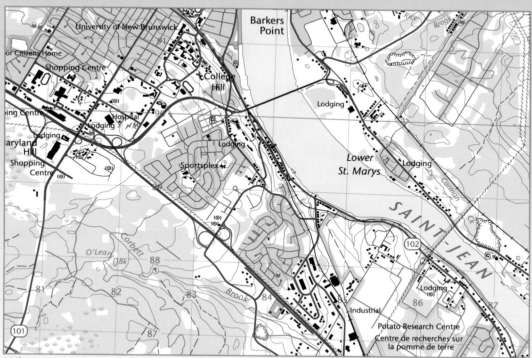

Hikers need to know whether their planned route up a mountain is a steep climb or a gently sloping path.

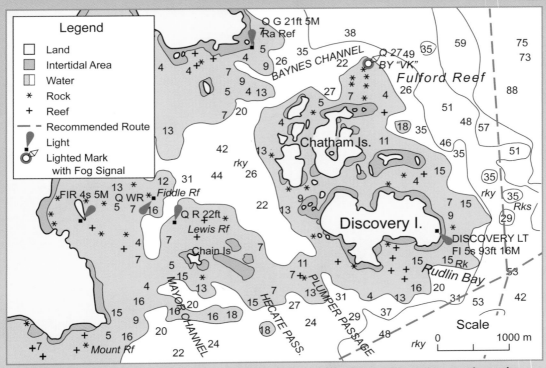

Legend

- ☐ Land
- ▨ Intertidal Area
- ▦ Water
- ∗ Rock
- + Reef
- – – Recommended Route
- 🚩 Light
- ⦿ Lighted Mark with Fog Signal

(Chart labels include: Q G 21ft 5M, Ra Ref, BAYNES CHANNEL, Q 2749 BY "VK", Fulford Reef, Chatham Is., Discovery I., DISCOVERY LT Fl 5s 93ft 16M, Rudlin Bay, FIR 4s 5M, Q WR, Fiddle Rf, Q R 22ft, Lewis Rf, Chain Is, MAYOR CHANNEL, HECATE PASS., PLUMPER PASSAGE, Mount Rf, rky, Rks, Rk, Scale 0 – 1000 m)

Divers and ship captains need to know how deep the water is, so that they can explore or pass through it safely.

Video and satellite images clearly show how the weather changes. But symbols like the ones to the right, which describe a cold front (blue) and a warm front (red), can show us what cameras can't capture.

(Satellite weather map labels: Maniwaki, Québec, Ottawa, Trois-Rivières, Peterborough, Montreal, Kingston, Toronto, don)

Colour

Colour can deliver information very quickly. On a map, meaning begins where you would expect it: blue for water, green for forests or parks, gold or pale yellow for prairie land.

Countries on a world map get contrasting colours so that it's easy to tell them apart. Even different shades of the same colour can give you information.

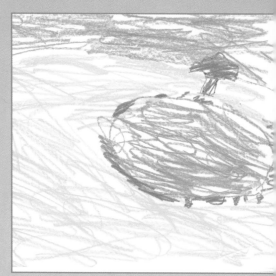

Ask your friends, "What is this a picture of?" and you'll find their answers are pretty much the same.

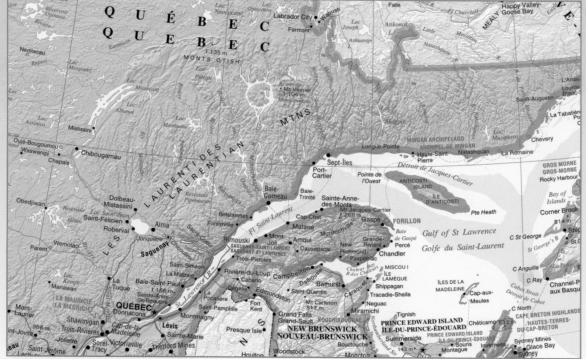

Shading is one way to show the shape of a place.

WORLD OF COLOUR

For a world map, you need at least five colours, so that no country is next to another of the same colour. But more more than thirteen colours on a single map is confusing.

A map can be a work of art.

Mapping Canada

The earliest known maps of Canada were drawn by seafaring explorers from Europe. Our whole continent was a surprise to them. When they found it, they were looking for something else — an easy passage to India and China. So early maps of North America highlight information useful to readers looking for a way through: the shape of coastlines, the location of waterways and how far they travelled into the land.

This early map shows what the explorers hoped: that the new lands were just a narrow strip between Europe and the silk and spices of the East.

FIRST KNOWLEDGE

Long before Europeans "discovered" Canada, many people already called this land home. Different groups lived on the richness of the land in familiar territories, travelling along established routes between their summer and winter homes. They had gathering places where strangers and friends met to celebrate and trade with one another.

European explorers and mapmakers throughout Canada depended on those First Nations' knowledge, which was kept and shared through stories, songs, marks on the landscape and drawings on bark or animal skin.

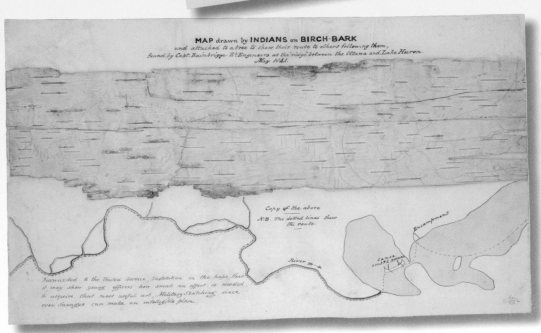

MAP drawn by INDIANS on BIRCH-BARK
and attached to a tree to shew their route to others following them,
found by Capt. Bainbrigge R.ᵉ Engineers at the ridge between the Ottawa and Lake Huron.
May 1841.

Copy of the above
N.B. The dotted lines shew the route.

River

Encampment

This map on birchbark shows a canoe route from the Ottawa and Mattawa Rivers to Lake Nippissing, in what is now Ontario.

15

Excited by news of the explorers' discoveries, Europe's mapmakers (or cartographers, as they're usually known) got to work. Since many of them had never seen the places they pictured, their maps weren't very accurate. But as interest in the new land grew, explorers collected more information, and the maps got better. Cartographers added rivers, lakes, forests, mountains, and named them. They outlined the territories of various First Nations and marked their villages, along with European forts, fishing ports and trading posts.

WHAT DO YOU CALL IT?

The word "map" comes from the Latin word *mappa*, meaning cloth. In earlier times, maps were drawn on animal skin or cloth. "Cartography" was borrowed from French: *cartographie* means "map drawing."

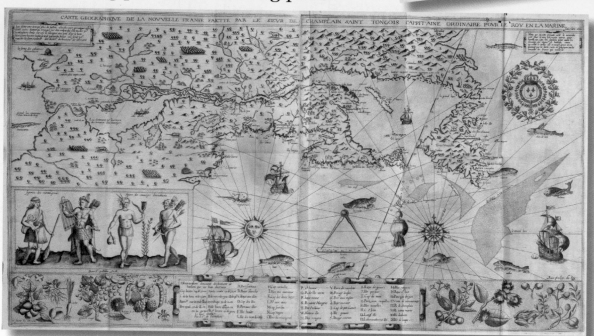

Explorer Samuel de Champlain published this map in 1612; it suggests how pleasant life might be in the New World.

NAMING IT

The First Nations gave our country — and our maps — something very important and lasting: names. Miramichi, Chicoutimi, Saskatchewan, Squamish, even Canada, are all names that come from First Nations languages.

European explorers renamed key places to honour the kings and queens who had sent them to explore. Even today, we sometimes rename places to show respect for a special person, people or event — like the Terry Fox Courage Highway near Thunder Bay, Ontario.

This section of Highway 401 in Ontario was renamed to honour Canadian soldiers.

WHERE IN THE WORLD?

Think about how you give directions — to a friend's house, for example:

Go up the River Street hill and turn left on Second Avenue. Go about half a block — I can't remember the number, but it's the white house with a big pine tree in front.

These directions involve measurements you can see (blocks); names you know (River Street, Second Avenue) and an obvious **landmark** ("big pine tree"). So far, so good.

But what happens if your listener is starting at the top of the River Street hill instead of the bottom, and has no clue what a pine tree looks like? Up becomes down, left becomes right . . . and which white house is it? You need two things to make sense of the confusion: **cardinal directions** and **orientation.**

This **compass rose** is located at a lookout point to help sightseers orient themselves. You will find something like this on any map.

WHIRLING WORLD

The sun doesn't really rise or set. Our planet spins, always presenting a new area to the sun while another is turned away — like a marshmallow at a campfire. Earth spins counterclockwise, so that sunrise in Canada starts on the east coast and moves west.

Cardinal Directions

East, West, North and South: the idea of cardinal directions is shared across world cultures and is very old. The directions are based on dependable, repeating features of life on our planet that people have been observing, describing and naming since the beginning of history: sunrise and sunset, the changing of the seasons, the stars in the sky.

East is the direction of the rising sun. In many languages, the word for east means, literally, "dawn." In Chinese, the word for east can also mean "spring" or "beginning."

West is the direction of the setting sun. In many languages, the word for west relates to evening and the things animals and people do in the evening: birds roosting, people resting.

In English, north may come from an earlier word that meant "left" — in other words, the direction on your left when you are facing the rising sun.

South, for Canadians and other people who live in the northern half of the planet, means sun and warmth. Homes are warmer and mountains more green with plant life on the south side.

Orientation

Imagine you are travelling in a strange place in the middle of the night, with no idea where the sun had set or where it might rise in the morning. How do you know which direction is which? How do you place yourself? Well, if it's a clear night, and you're in the northern half of the planet — in Canada, say — you could find your way by using the North Star.

As our planet travels around the sun, our view of space changes. So the stars we see in the night sky are a little different with each season. But one star remains "fixed," always in the same position relative to the Earth. That star is Polaris, or the North Star. Wherever we find Polaris in the night sky, that way is always north.

As our planet turns, the stars seem to change positions in the sky. A camera captures the movement as trails of light. In this photo, Polaris is the still point at the centre of the rings.

FIND THE NORTH STAR

To find Polaris in the night sky, first find the Big Dipper, then trace a line along the outer edge of the "pot" (farthest from the "handle"), from the bottom to the top. Keep going, and the first bright star you come to is the North Star. This star is also the tip of the Little Dipper's handle.

The first compass was a magnetized needle floating on water.

MAKE YOUR OWN COMPASS

To make this compass, you need a shallow dish of water, a cork or styrofoam disk, and a magnetized needle. To magnetize a needle, simply rub a magnet on it 15 times, always from top to tip. Lay the needle on the disk and place them on the water's surface. When it has settled into position, you will find that the head is pointing north.

But what if you are travelling in a strange place in the middle of a cloudy night? How do you place yourself then?

About two thousand years ago, the Chinese discovered **lodestone**, a natural magnet. If suspended and allowed to move freely, a lodestone would always point the same way, north-south. It took a few centuries, but eventually someone figured out that lodestone might be useful as a direction-finder, especially at sea, in unfamiliar waters or out of sight of land.

So the first recorded use of a **compass** — a north-south direction finder — was by a Chinese sailor, in the 12th century.

A compass rose on a map shows its orientation, so that you can find and give directions without confusion. No matter whether it's in front or behind you, north is always north. All you have to do is match up north on the map with north in real life.

Navigation

Early sailors were afraid of leaving sight of land. The open sea had no landmarks and with one storm they might be lost forever. With the compass, things started to change. The compass was the first **navigation** (way-finding) instrument that didn't depend on the sky or landmarks. Gradually, **navigators** developed other tools for measuring and recording their location.

Using instruments and cardinal directions alone, navigators invented a new way to describe location. They imagined our whole planet covered with invisible lines. They named the lines running around the Earth **latitude**, and the lines running from the North to the South Poles **longitude**, and numbered them. With these imaginary lines covering the globe, every place on Earth became the crossing point of one line running east-west and another running north-south.

Lines of latitude and longitude are called **degrees**. The areas between degrees are divided into smaller units called minutes and seconds.

compass

sextant

astrolabe

early ship's chronometer

With these instruments, navigators could figure out their north-south and east-west positions.

The crossing-points could be named using a pair of numbers called **co-ordinates**: one number for latitude, one for longitude. At last, travellers could identify and describe wherever they were, even on the open sea. It was as if every place on Earth had its own address, as specific as 34 River Street or 87 Second Avenue.

LOST AND FOUND

Land explorers in Canada also used navigation instruments. In 1613, the French explorer and cartographer Samuel de Champlain lost his astrolabe during a difficult portage in the Ottawa River area. In 1867, 14-year-old Edward Lee unearthed an astrolabe while helping his father clear trees from their farm by Green Lake, Ontario. Was it Champlain's? Historians are almost certain it was. Today, you can see the astrolabe at the Canadian Museum of Civilization in Ottawa.

Champlain's astrolabe

GPS Navigation

The newest instrument for travellers is the **GPS** (Global Positioning System) unit. You may have one in your family car. A GPS is like a map, a compass and a computer packed into one handy gadget. Here's how it works:

Like a map, a GPS unit holds and displays location information — longitude and latitude, and land features like roads and rivers, distances and directions.

A compass responds to the pull of Earth's magnetic North Pole, so you can use it to figure out where you are in relation to that one point, north. A GPS unit responds to radio signals, figuring out where it is in relation to satellites orbiting Earth.

TREASURE HUNT!

Geocaching is a worldwide treasure hunt using satellite technology. There are geocaches hidden in secret places all over the world. Players download location co-ordinates and clues from a geocaching website, and then go looking. Most often, they find a watertight container holding small toys, a logbook and a pencil. They note the date in the logbook and trade a toy from the cache with one they brought along. Then they hide the container again so it's ready for the next geocacher to find.

A computer uses mathematics and memory to make calculations and display information. A GPS calculates how far it is from each of three or more satellites. (The longer a signal takes to go out to and return from a satellite, the farther away it is.) Then the GPS compares those distances to figure out its own location. It displays that location using the map information it has in its memory.

As you travel, a GPS "navigator" keeps track of your location, showing you the map information it has for that location while guiding you to your destination.

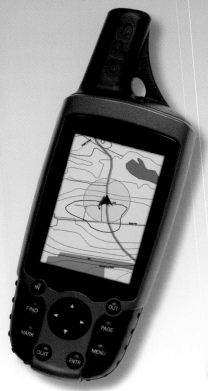

The location-finding method GPS uses is called triangulation.

A statue of David Thompson and Charlotte Small at Invermere, British Columbia

David Thompson

David Thompson was the greatest cartographer Canada has ever known. It is estimated that he personally mapped about twenty percent of the land in North America. In 1814, he produced a masterpiece, a map of the North American interior from the Fraser River to Lake Superior. It was so accurate that even one hundred years later, Canadian cartographers were still using it as a base for other maps.

David Thompson was born in Wales in 1770 and came to Canada when he was only fourteen years old, as an apprentice for the Hudson's Bay Company. For twenty years he travelled by foot and canoe, charting rivers, lakes and mountain passes that no cartographer had ever seen before.

David Thompson's masterpiece

One great help to Thompson was his wife, Charlotte Small, the daughter of a Cree mother and Scottish fur trader father. She often travelled with Thompson and used her understanding of the languages and customs of the First Nations people they met to smooth their way into unknown territory.

In spite of his great service to young Canada, David Thompson was ignored and living in great poverty when he died in 1857. Slowly, over the years, his achievements have been recognized, in memorials, statues — even a stamp. But the best place to look for David Thompson is on a map.

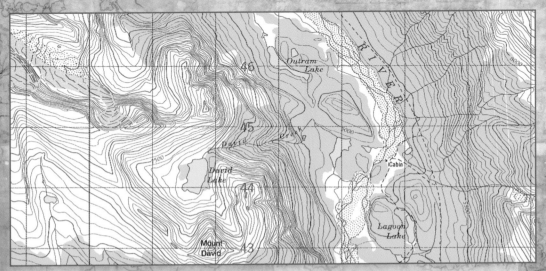

David Thompson travelled through this area near today's Banff National Park in 1807. This map shows three features named after him.

SIZING THINGS UP

While the earliest explorers in Canada were navigators, later explorers were surveyors.

Surveying is the detailed measurement of land and its features. Surveyors use mathematics and instruments that can pinpoint distance, height, angles and location (longitude and latitude). Anyone who owns land depends on a survey to tell them what, exactly, is theirs: from countries deciding where borders lie, to your parents deciding where to put a fence in your backyard.

Explorer-surveyors were sent, first by the big fur trade companies and then by the new government of the new country of Canada, to find out what, exactly, lay west of the Great Lakes. In Canada and the United States, they raced to find the quickest routes through the Rocky

An attractive survey plan can inspire people to move in and make a place their home. This neighbourhood for the growing city of Winnipeg, Manitoba, was planned around 1910.

Mountains to the Pacific Ocean, and to trace the paths of the West's great rivers. The information they collected and the maps they created helped Canada grow.

Even today, every time a new road is built or land is cleared for houses, surveyors are the first ones in, measuring, marking and mapping. The information that surveyors collect (called **data**) is brought back to the office and entered into a computer. A computer program adds the new data to existing information and helps turn it into exactly the kind of map road builders or developers need.

Survey data is also recorded on stakes, like this one.

MAKE YOUR OWN MAP

Maps are everywhere — in stores and libraries and schools, even in phone books. You can find a map on the Internet and print it instantly. So why make your own?

It's simple. Maps are all about information, and everybody on the planet has a different set of information in their heads. Getting from A to B is one thing, but you might have some special knowledge about A, B or the route between them that you want to share. A map is a great way to do it.

Information changes, too. Maps get old — and they aren't always correct to start with. If you live in a new neighbourhood in a city or suburb, or in the country on a quiet road, chances are you'll find mistakes in the maps of your area.

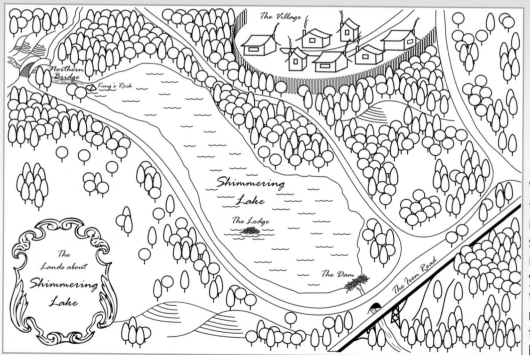

With an imaginative map (and some renaming!), you can turn your neighbourhood into a fantasy land.

THE CHALLENGER RELIEF MAP

In 1947, George Challenger began a project that he hoped would make kids feel as proud of British Columbia as he did. For seven years, he cut, sanded, painted and glued. The result? An awe-inspiring **topographic** map of the province that covered 1,850 square metres (6,070 square feet) and was named in *The Guinness Book of Records* as the largest map of its kind in the world. The Challenger Relief Map was on display at the Pacific National Exhibition in Vancouver until 1997 and is now awaiting a new, permanent home.

The Callenger Map, made up of 986,000 pieces of fir plywood, shows all of British Columbia's topographical features — mountains, valleys, rivers and lakes — in exact scale. Each layer of wood represents 76.2 vertical metres (250 vertical feet).

And maps are works of art, don't forget. Colour, symbols and design can all say something special about a place, and the way you feel about it.

Visitors stand on a special platform to view the map.

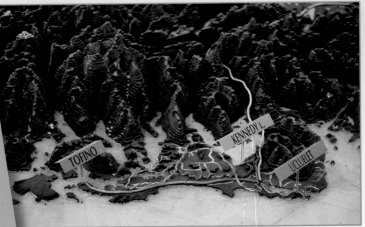

A small portion of Vancouver Island from the Challenger map

Making a Map

Step I: Plan

A map begins with a detailed plan. First, you need to brainstorm a few things:

Who is my map for?

What information do I want them to see first?

What area is the map going to show?

How big is the map going to be?

What features need to appear on the map?

How is the map going to be displayed?

Once the details are clear in your mind, you'll have a better idea of how your map should look. Then you can begin collecting data.

- for friends
- directions
- neighbourhood
- 20 cm X 25 cm
- route, Carsons' dog, swamp, poison ivy, climbing tree
- paper

REAL WORLD MAPPING 1

These are the questions all cartographers ask themselves when planning to make a map.

Step 2: Research

Let's say you're making a map of your neighbourhood, showing a shortcut you've discovered between your house and a friend's. You could walk the route with a metre wheel, tape measure, compass and camera, taking pictures and notes as you go.

There are other ways to start, though. You can look for a map on the Internet or in the library that is similar to the one you're planning and use it as a **base map** for your own. If you want to trace an existing map, you'll have to make sure it's at a scale you want.

If you're starting with an existing map, you'll still need to walk your route with a copy in hand, ready to correct or add information as needed.

If you have a GPS unit and know how to use it, you can mark key locations on your route: the start and finish points, and the locations of things such as unfriendly dogs, a muddy patch or some poison ivy — whatever you want the map reader to know about.

33

Step 3: Draw

You can draw your map like the pros do, using a computer. Drawing programs such as Adobe Illustrator or Corel Draw let you scan an existing map, then trace it as a base for your own map. Such programs also have symbols and different line and type styles to help you build your map.

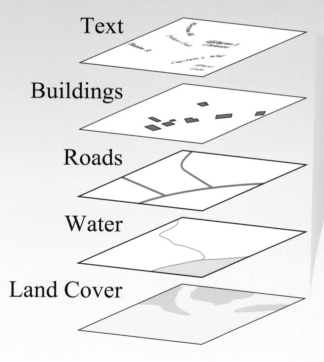

Text

Buildings

Roads

Water

Land Cover

Mary Anne Rd.

Professor Creek

Gilligan's Corners

Thurston St.

Captain's Way

Ginger Lake

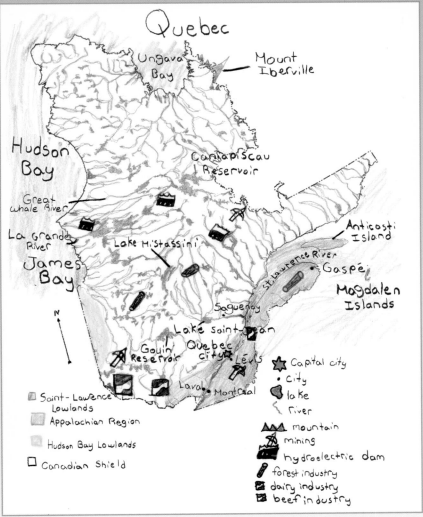

There's nothing wrong with good old-fashioned paper and pencil, though. Graph paper will help you with scale. When placing information on your map, don't forget to make it look good, using colours, symbols, different line thicknesses and styles, and lettering. Leave room for the special map features you want to include: a north arrow or compass rose, a legend or a scale bar.

SHOWING WHAT WE KNOW

The days of exploring are done — on Earth's surface, anyway. There's still plenty we don't know about the bottom of the sea, about caves and, of course, about space. And no doubt there are places where you haven't been that you'll want to explore for yourself someday.

But today, we're able to look at the world very precisely in many ways, and have on hand an enormous amount of data about it. Everything on Earth has a place, and with GPS and an Internet connection, everything — hurricanes, traffic, radio-tagged wildlife, even your friends if they have cell phones — can be tracked at all times.

WORLD OF MAPS

A program like Google Earth gives you a virtual globe that you can spin around and zoom in on, to peer at the details provided by satellite and air photos. You can also use it to display 3-dimensional landscapes and buildings. There are even some games that allow you to fly an airplane or drive a car around the planet.

Using Google mapping tools, you can "fly" through one of Canada's national parks.

All that information is precisely why we still need maps. The more we know about a place, the more important a good map becomes. A good map shows the reader the most information with the least amount of confusion. Maps today are about understanding not so much the where, but the what, how and why of a place and the people who live in it.

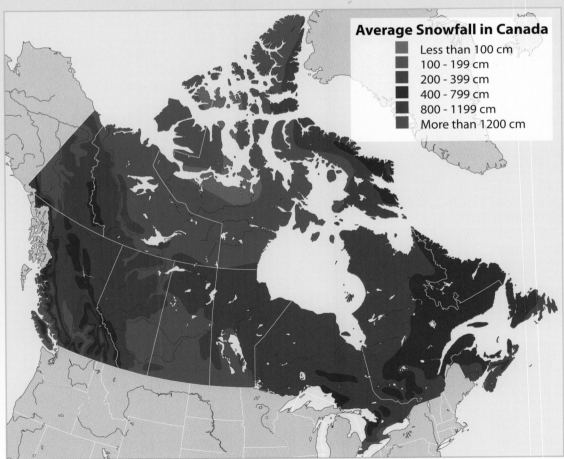

Average Snowfall in Canada
- Less than 100 cm
- 100 - 199 cm
- 200 - 399 cm
- 400 - 799 cm
- 800 - 1199 cm
- More than 1200 cm

If you love snow, where are the best places in Canada to be? This map gives you an answer with just one look.

Glossary

base maps
maps used as information sources for creating other maps

cardinal directions
directions based on planet Earth and its movements; north, east, south and west

colour
characteristic of a map that conveys information while looking good to the eye

compass
direction-finding tool that uses Earth's magnetism to point out north-south

compass rose
feature on a map that shows how it is oriented

contour lines
symbol system on a map for showing height on land

co-ordinates
pairs of numbers that describe location

data
information

degrees
units of division in measuring latitude and longitude

GPS
global positioning system; a device that communicates with satellites orbiting Earth to determine location

landmark
feature of the landscape that helps you identify a location

latitude
system of imaginary lines encircling planet Earth; a north-south section of Earth

legend
feature of a map that shows what its symbols mean

lodestone
naturally magnetic rock

longitude
system of imaginary lines running between Earth's north and south poles; an east-west section of Earth

navigation
way-finding

navigators
sailors or others whose job is to find the way

orientation
position relative to planet Earth

proportions
relation of size between different objects or within an object

relative
compared or in relation (to another, similar thing)

scale
size of a map relative to the actual place the map pictures

scale bar
feature of a map that shows its scale

surveying
measuring land and its features

symbols
shapes, lines, dots or icons on a map that represent something in the world

topographic
showing the shape of the physical landscape, including hills, valleys and landcover

Longitude

Latitude